new by date own.

Tell ME What YOU Remember

CLOTHES

Sarah Ridley

W
FRANKLIN WATTS
LONDON · SYDNEY

Franklin Watts
First published in Great Britain in 2015 by
The Watts Publishing Group

Series editor: Sarah Peutrill
Series design: Basement68

The Author and Publisher would
like to thank everyone who has
kindly contributed their photos
and memories to this book.

Dewey classification: 391'.00941'0904
HB ISBN: 978 1 4451 3876 3
Library Ebook ISBN: 978 1 4451 3977 7

Printed in China

Franklin Watts
An imprint of
Hachette Children's Group
Part of The Watts Publishing Group
Carmelite House
50 Victoria Embankment
London EC4Y 0DZ

An Hachette UK Company
www.hachette.co.uk

www.franklinwatts.co.uk

Picture credits: Ted Dearberg/
IWM: 8,9,11tr. Evening Standard/
Hulton Archive/Getty Images: 17t.
Henry Grant/MOL/Getty Images:
front cover b,15b. Roy Jones/
Hulton Archive/Getty Images: 15t.
Willy Maywald/Keystone/Getty
Images: 12. NA/SSPL/Getty
Images: 10. Pictorial Press/Alamy:
17b. PMYCA/Alamy: 18.
Richard Pohl/The Times/Corbis:
19b. Popperfoto/Getty Images:
13b. Tim Roney/Hulton Archive/
Getty Images: 19t, 23b.
wavebreakmedia/Shutterstock:
4. All other photographs are
kindly given by the people who
contributed their memories.

Contents

Clothes   4

Baby Clothes   6

Clothes Rationing   8

Making and Mending   10

The 1940s and 50s   12

The 1960s   14

The 1970s   16

1980s Onwards   18

Dressed for the Occasion   20

School Uniform   22

Timeline   23

Glossary and Index   24

Clothes

What are your favourite clothes? Do you like to choose the clothes you wear? What do you wear on special occasions?

We wear cool clothes in summer, warm clothes in winter, sports clothes to run around in and swimsuits for the pool or the beach. Fashions change from year to year. It has always been like that.

Memories are what we remember about the past. Everyone has different memories about the clothes they wore when they were younger. Talking to people about what they remember can help us to learn about the past.

Katie, born 1991, remembers...

This photo was taken during the summer of 1998. I loved this dress and wore it as often as possible.

Sue, born 1945, remembers...

I'm the one who is winning in this photo taken at school in 1953. At my junior school, girls always wore a dress or a gymslip while boys wore shorts.

Baby Clothes

When your great-grandparents were babies, most of their clothes were made from white cotton. They could be washed in hot water using strong chemicals to get them clean. During the 1940s, more and more mothers dressed their boys in pale blue clothes and their girls in pale pink.

This photo was taken in 1938 and shows a baby boy wearing a dress. It was easy to lift up the dress to change the baby's nappy. Many mothers continued to dress baby boys in dresses through the 1940s and 1950s.

Jane, born 1963, remembers...

Here I am with my twin sister. Our mother bought most of our clothes from shops but knitted cardigans for us. Our baby clothes had to leave space for bulky cloth nappies.

My daughter Katie (below) was born in 1991. There was a huge choice of baby clothes in the shops. I dressed her in a babygro at night and dungarees and colourful outfits in the daytime.

FIND OUT MORE

Find a photo of you as a baby. Compare the clothes in your photo with the photos on these pages.

Clothes Rationing

During the Second World War (1939–1945), clothing factories needed to make uniforms, parachutes and other things for the war. Clothing became scarce. To share out clothes fairly, the government introduced clothes rationing. Everyone was given a Clothing Book, a book full of coupons.

In 1943, parents had to pay 16 shillings and give seven coupons to a shopkeeper to buy the shirt and shorts this boy is wearing.

FIND OUT MORE

Look for clues that tell you this photo was taken during the war. He is standing in front of a Morrison air-raid shelter – how did his family use it? Can you find the box containing his gas mask? Why did he need one?

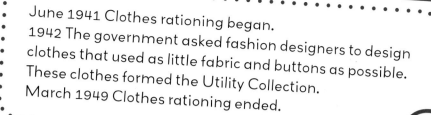

June 1941 Clothes rationing began.
1942 The government asked fashion designers to design clothes that used as little fabric and buttons as possible. These clothes formed the Utility Collection.
March 1949 Clothes rationing ended.

Jessie, born 1940, remembers...

My older sister wore this dress before I did. It was made by a dressmaker in the village. My mother knitted us jumpers and cardigans.

At clothing exchanges, mothers could bring in clothes and shoes that their children had outgrown and exchange them for something in a bigger size.

Making and Mending

During the Second World War women were asked to 'Make-do and Mend'. They learnt to cut out patterns, mend clothes and make new clothes out of old ones. Even when there were plenty of clothes to buy in the 1950s and 1960s, women often made their own to save money.

This wartime poster encouraged women to mend their clothes or even make a new dress for a child out of a worn out dress.

Go through your wardrobe

Make-do and Mend

Women learned how to sew and make clothes during this dressmaking class held in 1943. Find the girl who is learning to sew alongside her mother.

Irene, born 1939, remembers...

My grandma was a dressmaker and she always made clothes for us in the 1940s and 1950s. She never made them how we wanted them, or even how my mother wanted them!

FIND OUT MORE

Does anyone in your family sew, knit or mend clothes? Where did they learn their skills?

The 1940s and 50s

There was not much fabric or money around after the war and into the early 1950s. Many people continued to wear clothes in the Utility style that used as little fabric as possible. Others wanted to try out the new fashions that became popular.

Fashion designer Christian Dior introduced a fresh new style in 1947. The full skirt in this photo used much more fabric than wartime fashions.

1947 Christian Dior showed his new collection – the 'New Look'.
1950s The Teddy Boy style spread from London to the rest of the country.
1950s Teenagers started to wear clothes and hairstyles that were different from adults.

Annie, born 1949, remembers...

I had just learned to walk when this photo was taken. My coat and my mother's clothes are in the wartime Utility style that used as little fabric as possible.

Teddy Boys, like these teenage boys in 1955, wore narrow trousers and ties and long jackets.

FIND OUT MORE

You can try to work out when a photo was taken by looking at styles of hair and clothing.

13

The 1960s

During the 1960s clothes became fun, especially for young people. Fashion shops opened up all across the country. Girls and young women wore shift dresses and skirts got shorter and shorter. Many young men dressed like The Beatles or became Mods or Rockers.

Fans of the pop group, The Beatles, loved the clothes they wore as well as their music. Many young men bought clothes like theirs.

FIND OUT MORE

Ask people in your family to show you photos of what they wore in the 1960s.

Sue, born 1945, remembers...

I was a student in London in the 1960s. We all wore shift dresses and mini skirts, like the girls in this photo. My parents looked a bit shocked when I visited them for the weekend wearing a mini skirt!

Mods wore their hair neat and went out wearing smart suits and polished shoes. Some of them owned scooters and protected their clothes with long parka coats.

The first Biba fashion store opened in 1964. In 1964 Mary Quant designed the mini skirt. Skirts were at their shortest around 1967.

The 1970s

Through the 1970s, many styles came and went. In the early 1970s, hippy clothes were popular but so were hot pants, which were very short shorts. Young women wore mini skirts as well as longer maxi skirts. In the 1970s, men and women wore wide, flared trousers often with tight, fitted tops.

Yvonne, born 1968, remembers...

I got this dress as a present for my sixth birthday. Flower patterns like this were very popular in the seventies.

1971 Platform shoes and hot pants became fashionable.
1972 Nike trainers with the famous tick design went on sale.
1976 Punk fashions began to appear.

Men and women wore platform shoes, with high heels. This photo taken in 1973 shows a man wearing flared trousers and platform shoes. By the end of the 1970s, most people were wearing narrow trousers or jeans.

Funda, born 1968, remembers...

Fans of the Scottish pop group, the Bay City Rollers, liked to wear tartan clothes like the musicians in the band. I even had some tartan socks that I wore with my school uniform!

FIND OUT MORE

Look at the Bay City Rollers photo. What kind of shoes are they wearing?

1980s Onwards

Since the 1980s, several fashion styles have existed at the same time. In the 1980s, some people started to wear sport clothes all day long, a style that continues today. Tracksuits were made from polyester and leggings from stretchy fabrics which included lycra.

These teenagers wore tracksuits at a hip-hop event in 1986. One of them has brought along his ghetto blaster, used to listen to cassette tapes or radio stations.

Teenage girls copied the clothes worn by pop stars such as the Spice Girls, photographed here in 1996.

Eliza, born 1999, remembers...

I follow fashion in magazines and on Facebook. I buy my clothes online as well as in shops where they sell many different styles at once and are always bringing in new clothes to tempt me.

Through the 1980s and 1990s, a lot of women wanted to look like Princess Diana. In 2011 her son, Prince William, married Kate Middleton, right, who was given the title Duchess of Cambridge. People began to copy her look too.

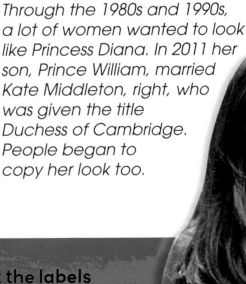

FIND OUT MORE

Look at the labels inside your clothes to find out what they are made from. The development of new fabrics has inspired fashion designers over the years.

Dressed for the Occasion

When you look at old photos you have to remember that often the photo records a special day. People are wearing their best clothes rather than the clothes they wore every day.

This wedding photo was taken in 1965. Who is wearing hats or gloves? Do people wear cotton gloves today?

Judith, born 1947, remembers...

The whole country was excited about Queen Elizabeth II's coronation in 1953. Our village celebrated by holding a children's tea party and a fancy dress competition. This is the dress my mother made for me.

On 7 June 1977 it was time to celebrate Queen Elizabeth II's Silver Jubilee. Street parties took place all over the country. People wore their best clothes. Look carefully at how the children are dressed in this photo.

School Uniform

What do you wear to school? Most schoolboys growing up between the 1930s and the 1960s wore a wool jacket or blazer with a shirt, shorts or trousers. Girls wore a gymslip over a blouse in winter and a cotton dress in the summer.

A 1950s schoolboy

Annie, born 1949, remembers...

I wore a navy-blue gymslip over a white cotton blouse at junior school and we were not allowed to wear trousers. On cold days, I wore a wool cardigan knitted by my mother.

During the 1960s and 70s some schools allowed children to wear their own clothes but uniforms have remained popular to this day.

22

Timeline

Use this timeline to see at a glance some of the information in this book.

1930s Baby boys often wore dresses.

1940s Wartime clothes rationing. The Utility Collection was designed. Shops started selling many more 'blue for boys', 'pink for girls' clothes.

1947 The 'New Look' was designed by Christian Dior.

1950s Teenagers wanted to develop their own styles, such as those worn by Teddy Boys.

1964 Mary Quant designed the mini skirt. Mods and Rockers developed their own styles.

Late 1960s/early 1970s Hippy clothes were popular.

1970s Mini skirts and maxi skirts were worn by women. Platform shoes were popular, as were clothes made from colourful printed fabrics.

Mid-1970s Wide bell-bottom trousers became popular. Tartan clothes became popular because of the Bay City Rollers pop group. Punk fashion spreads from London.

1980s Sportswear and leggings made from polyester and lycra became very popular.

1980s–1990s Many women copied Princess Diana's style.

1990s Teenage girls wanted to wear clothes like their favourite pop stars, including the Spice Girls.

2010 onwards Many women copied the Duchess of Cambridge's style.

Today Many fashion styles exist at the same time.

Glossary

Coronation The ceremony when a king or queen is crowned.

Coupon A slip of paper torn out of a ration book.

Fashion Style or design popular at a particular time.

Gas mask Face mask that protects people against poison gas.

Hip-hop Style of popular music that began in the 1980s.

Hippy Name given to people who want to look different and follow alternative lifestyles.

Mods In the early 1960s, young people called Mods wore smart clothes, rode scooters and listened to soul music.

Morrison air-raid shelter A strong metal cage that families sheltered in during an air raid. It also served as a dining table.

Patterns Paper sewing patterns used to make clothes.

Ration book A book containing coupons that were cut out or stamped by a shopkeeper when someone wanted to buy rationed goods.

Shift A simple dress style popular in the 1960s.

Shillings Coins used in the UK at this time. There were 20 shillings in one pound.

Silver Jubilee In 1977 Queen Elizabeth II celebrated 25 years on the throne.

Teddy Boys In the 1950s, groups of young men called Teddy Boys wore narrow trousers, swept up hair styles and listened to rock-and-roll music.

Utility Collection Well-designed clothes that used as little fabric and other materials as possible.

Index

baby clothes 6–7
Bay City Rollers 17

clothes rationing 8–9
Coronation, the 21

Dior, Christian 12
dressmakers 9, 11
Duchess of Cambridge 19

flared trousers 16–17

hairstyles 12–13, 15
hip-hop 18
hippy clothes 16

knitting 7, 9, 11, 22

Make-do and Mend 10–11
mini skirts 14–16
Mods 14–15

Punks 17

Second World War 8–13
sewing 9–11
shoes, platform 17
Silver Jubilee 21
Spice Girls 19
sportswear 4, 18

Teddy Boys 12–13
The Beatles 14

uniform, school 5, 22
Utility Collection 9, 12–13